On Kevin's Boat

On Kevin's Boat

and Other Poems

Deborah Paes de Barros

BLUE WEST BOOKS
RIVERSIDE, CALIFORNIA

Blue West Books
Riverside, California

Copyright © 2013, Deborah Paes De Barros
All rights reserved
Printed in the United States of America
First edition, 2013

The following poems in this collection were previously published: "Boom Vang" in *Barbaric Yawp*, "Disorder in Kansas and Guatemala" in *California Quarterly*, "Andrea's Wedding" and "Van Gogh's Haystacks" in *San Diego Annual 2012*, "My Mother's Parrot" in *San Diego Annual 2008*, "When the Sardines Run" and "Cologne" in *Arsenic Lobster*, and "When the Sardines Run" in *Best of Arsenic Lobster 2008*.

ISBN: 978-0-9859495-1-8
LCCN: 20129119532

Blue West Books is a publishing collective dedicated to promoting emerging and established authors of contemporary fiction, poetry, and essays in California and the Southwest.

www.BlueWestBooks.com

For Carlton—mariner of more than ordinary oceans
and seas I would never have seen—love

Contents

III The Four Oaks at the End of the Mind

IV My Mother's Parrot

On Kevin's Boat

I When the Sardines Run

On Kevin's Boat

On Kevin's boat brass gleams
    in yellow sun as
    a woman and her relatives visiting from Iowa
    climb aboard and
    someone helps an elderly lady up a top step.
    She sits now on a polished oak seat,
    faces backward,

ten minutes calls a man from the deck.

There are eleven people on this boat but
    Kevin yells back there's still more room.
    And even after the white bowline springs free
    an angular blond woman runs down the dock
    certain there's always space.

And there is.

We motor out of the broad harbor.
    all salt and gasoline
    and the hulls of pale moored yachts,

    out beyond breakwater and a last thin neck of land

    then the wide sails open and catch
    like vast white wings on some gigantic
    and lovely lost bird

water bigger than memory and refractive as new glass.

Later we eat from a plate of cracked crab and
    crackers, brown bottles of beer and gingersnaps.
    We know now how the sea shifts

---

blue in one place, then black

      last night I dreamed I was on a boat
      a man I barely recognized lay down beside me.
      Suddenly I was fifteen, remembered
      how the Russian River pours out
      the coldness of all that water, thick with ancient silt
      rivers or streams, yearning always to become one;

      all the years people live stringing leaves together
      dreaming always that word: ocean

      the way we linked fingers once to
      walk in the dark-

on Kevin's boat we are webbed together;
we know this,
sailing past the broad beach and
the rocky point just north of Cayucos
finger of black pier and fishing boats,

we are slipping always toward the horizon
that thin line penciled across sight.

My hip presses against a woman who sits by me.
      We ride together, all of us,

      swathed in light, watch the remote shades of land,
      recall as the boat rocks and tips faint spray that

      this is where we were born.

When the Sardines Run Again

On that day the sardines moved as a single wave,
        as a gull's wing, breaking the surface of water,
mercurial, beacons flickering
again and again,

like a silver we have heard of
but no longer believe in.

Later, on the beach, after we left the pier,
an old surfer told us that
        he had seen this before—
how the sardines turned the sea into pale swathes of silver,
        how when he spread his palms wide
his hands came up filled with light,
and the fish swam thick around his torso
        marking him too with silver.

The next day people talked about the heavy flocks of birds
        following the fish.
Everyone had a story.
Some even saw smooth gray whales in the wake
and one man photographed porpoises.

But all this seems inconsequential.
For us it will always be the thin silver fish.
It shouldn't have been possible anymore
how they charged the water around that silent, solitary pier.

And long after, if things were difficult
  or only different

we talked about how the sea swelled silver
  slapping against the pilings,

sardines dancing in atavistic return.

Boom Vang

Later people would tell us
  that we resembled a vast broken winged bird,
  sails crumpled in upon themselves
  collected wind twisted in taut pockets of canvas,
  whirling us across green space.
 They told us how they
  winced watching, our bow
  threading through the moored yachts,
  rudder cracked, lines snapping loose and
  our hands waving in the air in some forgotten
  language.

  If you'd been going the right way, people said later,
  you would have won the race.

But it seemed to me then that the boat finally found
  what it wanted always to be:

  dancer liberated from choreography,
  the great sheets of sail free to furl or not,
  to pirouette across water.
  No worrying about right of way, or
  how my father would have said to do things,
  or even simple chores
  like the right way to cook tomatoes and

  even the pack of harbor seals howled at how
  reckless it is to move free.

I've always liked November days like that one,
  wind hard and cold
  from off shore, clear as new bone,
  whole world just invented

like the day when I was seventeen
and first fell in love.

We had no business going out that day,

disregarding warning and
missing with one pure turn
the steel side of a disintegrating barge.

Sometimes I think it's all just luck.

That one moment in late autumn,
an otter cracked clams against his chest, made the
sound of a fog horn, low throated
as a man after making love

and later, seated around dark walnut tables,
all of us talking about such a near miss,
drinking red wine, all

I could think was

just for once we'd broken
free.

Meriwether Lewis

In that moment, finally, when he saw the sea

        —a vast slice of blue
        how it went on forever—

he sat down on the sand, let
the white powder trickle through his fingers
        and then slowly untied his boots.

In the water his feet were numb,
he could see them
        like pale fish swimming in what was now green.

The sea was worth everything.

That was his problem, of course,
        how he'd never thought of anything after the sea,
        how just seeing it was sufficient.
His friend Clark made sketches in his notebook,
        inventoried it all,
        knew you could parlay such things into a future.
But when the sea is everything there's no trade possible.

This is why he drank later,
        raw, southern bourbon,
        lay in his fetid bunk in St. Louis,
        blotting it all out,
        or trying.
Because nothing else would ever measure up.

The way the sea is now to certain people,
        the bend in the shore and
        the way the yellow hills reach down,

---

and the water washes up smooth rock
and old pieces of glass.
The way you remember the sound at night.

People talked as they do. Disgraceful they said
to waste all that opportunity.
A kind of treason of the spirit.

This is what some people always say.

Tossing on his grimy mattress
he tried to recall the precise geometry of space,
        the long road, the gorge and
        then, always then, the sea.
It beat against his brain
even when he could not completely remember,
        like a song thinly etched on the mind.
He drained the bottle then
felt feebly for the flask he'd hidden.

After that day everything fell into blankness
no reason to keep going.

He knew though that only fools found it finally sad.

A hundred shades of blue
imprinted on the inside of his eyelids

        he had after all made it to the ocean.

The Drowning

When they came to my door I told them the truth:

> we met just five weeks before when
> there was a dance in the dormitory courtyard.

He stood behind a small fountain
> the water turned off, fetid plants of a luminous green
> grew from the damp, he held
> a plastic cup of cheap wine in his hand.

Later we went back to my room.
We stopped on the third floor landing

> he pressed the hard planes of his face against mine,
> rough jaw, and the clean long line of his cheekbone.

That's all there was really.
Two other nights he came back.

Last Saturday in the afternoon he sat
> with his friends on the rocks by the breakwater,
> way out past the bay.

At least this is what I've heard.

I've often gone there myself, listened to the ocean,
> to the relentless echo, loud like
> stones smashing or
> like the sudden sound the glass made, breaking—
> he made a quick movement with his arm,
> knocked it from the stand by the bed.

They called it a rogue wave.

———

People tried to save him.
One man even plunged into the sea himself, but

the wave moved upward from the ocean bottom
a vast molten substance,
all green and inexorable.

I believe he recognized it when it came;

he had been waiting a long time.

Even when he held me on the stairwell
he waited.

Everyone asks me questions. His mother
wrote me a note.
I lie on my cotton sheets and think of his salty skin
how thirsty he always was—
that's why the glass was by the bed and

I have nothing left to say.

5 Days Before the Equinox: Real Estate Tips

In 23 years an asteroid will hit the earth,
        its fiery tail blazing then into black.

The real estate agent tells me this
        as we sit signing dense documents.
She holds a particular type of calculator
I wonder if she calculates time and mass.
Her porcelain nails tap the table—23 years she says,
        well, good I think, 30 year mortgage
        already shortened.

Today the globe is tipping slightly
        a subtle falling forward into still warm sky,
        near autumn now, I feel it
        that small juxtaposition of ground and pale space.

Later in a dim café
        we order eggplant sandwiches.
        I hold my wine glass
        catching thin shards of faded light,
        Talk about my mother,
        after seeing a lawyer, making a trust
        she lay tiredly on her bed, patted my hand, said
        it's for your beach house.
        In the months she's been gone
        I too plummet, free falling.

I tell you about the asteroid,
        how it will shorten our indebtedness, and you smile.
        Even now it powers down towards us,
        its electric pull marks our skin.
        Earth turns slowly away from sun,
        five days left before fall.

It may be that it's all about trust.

Across from us a woman—
        dark ringlets, 3 kids, reads a flyer on property sales.
        Are you buying, she asks.
We say we might, and she cites interest rates telling us
        it's a good time to buy.
        I think of the texture a cool birch wood floor
        and wonder if I should tell the woman
        about the potential astral collision.

My mother collected glass animals—
        made in France by Lalique, a butterfly and a fish.
        Outside now on this beach the jade and cobalt sea
        glass tumbles, left maybe
        from some other asteroid.

We make offers. Even without calculators
        we derive numbers and facts.
It is all a kind of calculus
        and incalculable.
Everyone on holiday, this weekend in a beach town,
        days dissolving,
        on notice now, the asteroid is coming.

We want something perfect
        something to withstand fire and water
        or loss.

Timing is everything says a man eating a pizza.
I'm inclined to agree.
At night I will lie in my bed and wonder exactly
how many years it takes a star to fall.

It is almost the equinox.

II Colony Collapse

Disorder in Kansas and Guatemala

The bees are leaving, waving their thin wings and flying,
        no one knows where.
I read about it in the newspaper
twenty-five percent of the bees gone already,
        just since October,
the beekeepers in white veils bereft, looking into deserted
hives and apiaries.
There's a name for this: colony collapse disorder,
        in Guatemala, Brazil and Kansas
        a rapture of bees rising steadily skyward.
No one knows why.

Late at night I open a cupboard,
        spoon honey on to a pale blue plate.
I plan to buy more, hide it for some future day
Putting the jar away and washing my fingers,
        I think of two women I know.
        I think they are like the bees.
One hacked at her flesh for a while, then
        made a phone call. The other swallowed a vial
        of white pills, prayed for oblivion.
Today though they tell me it's simply a kind of
        bio-chemical disarray, easily balanced,
        easily made right,
        a kind of pharmaceutical misunderstanding.
I saw one woman dancing a few months ago,
        supple as grass
        then she collapsed laughing on a pillow on the floor.
She was drinking sweet wine.
Still she weeps secretly,
        doesn't sleep. In the hospital she couldn't have
        flowers in a vase
        because of what she might do with the

shards of glass.
The other woman blames everything on her face,
     says it's not the kind of face to find love.
We walked on the beach once,
she told me she was from Iowa,
     the youngest of five.
     Her sisters have hair the color of corn.
     All married.

The flowering pear tree in my yard
hums with the sound of bees,
far too many to count, though I try.
I don't want to lose one.
All the shiny leaves and white blossoms,
who knows what disturbs the bees—
     maybe some digital transmission, or
     a genetically modified corn flower.
The white hives disrupted,

the bees cannot understand,
they used to dance their way home,
now they fly off without direction
into the cacophonous black night.
They tire of the infinite morphology of science.
The bees want order, need it,

even if it requires a death.

The Pink Lady of Adelaida

She dances in a long gown.
The moon grows ivory and spent—nineteen, wife
        of a Mennonite minister
he makes her wear her pretty hair up.

It is the endless dust that finishes her finally
        the way the wind always blows, married at sixteen,
        two babies dead, tender skin
        marked with traces of silver
        white powder from the mercury mine.

Just leave it to God, says her husband,
        leave it she endlessly repeats,
writing her name in the dust that lines the enameled plates
her mother's good china from Ohio all long gone.

After the babies die she asks for flowers.
The man with his skinny throat talks to her
        of the hereafter.

Sometimes she dreams of a clean-shirted young man.
He teaches her to dance.
        She thinks about the way his palm opens to her,
        She steps with one foot, then slides with another.

Her husband finds her once moving in the makeshift kitchen
hair quite wild, dressed in a night shift
        I am trying to learn to waltz she says.
        Can you not even keep time?

Three days later she lies dead
Poison say some, her small
        body draped over the graves of her girls.

———

Years pass. The mine closes.
Impossible to drink the water.

Visitors to the old cemetery see her still.
She dances and carries wild roses.
Listen to me she calls to the young girls—
      who ride late in the night with their teenage lovers
      hands on the boys' thighs, cigarettes glowing—
      Listen to me.

She raises the hem of her gown, shakes off the dirt
white fingers held upward.

Listen to me.
She dances on their graves,
throws stones at her adolescent visitors.

Fuck them all, she says.

Van Gogh's Haystacks

Straw the color of gold lies in sheaves along the road
    just east of Highway 1,
    loose bits piled in the field,
most of the hay rolled into vast wheels of sun
    burning through the summer fog.
Above it all Montana de Oro, its top obscured

I climbed that hill three years ago and saw
    a rattlesnake eat a lizard. The snake, mouth full,
    threw its head back and shook its kill
    like some prehistoric reptile in a book.
    Two women told me they saw two other striped snakes,
    enough for me, and I climbed back down.

Now I stick to the beach.
But I'm back today, feet covered in
faded vines and yellow weed
    field almost molten.

Years ago I took art history—because a boyfriend did
    notes written with care on lined yellow pads,
    the qualities of brush stroke
    and stylistic definition. He never missed class—
    he was like that, a
    lawyer now somewhere. If I saw him I would ask

do you remember

    that night at the beach?
    Can you still recite the qualities of Expressionism?
    His voice would be nervous.
    His mother served me cherries and kiwi fruit
    before they were fashionable.

———

A dusky twilight hung in the auditorium,
    the click of the projector,
     sometimes the urge to sleep irresistible,
     I put my head down on my arm,
     almost everything a steady drone of
     words and thin light.
Do you remember that night at the beach?

I imagine a brush stroke feels
like the light touch of a lover, the movement of
    a lock of hair against a bare shoulder.
I remember the color of light,
     clouds and the way sky stretched endlessly blue
     the stacking of straw.
And now, today, I have found it.

Haystacks of gold,
    Like all the other things forgotten
As real, and as tangible as skin itself.

I Dreamt of Ruth

Waking in the early morning
sky still gray and wet, ocean opaque
as it is so often here by the sea in the summer,
I put on a sweater, brew coffee.

We lived on the Westside then,
      across the street from each other
      with our babies, in buildings
      with wrought iron and patios
      thick with bougainvillea,
talked about novels
     and men.

   Once we went fishing for trout, then lit candles, ate pesto
    and later pistachios with cream—

In the dream I live in a large house, mostly glass
at the top of a high hill overlooking the Pacific.
A couple moved in across the road,
      displacing the two bony meth addicts who'd taped
      newspaper over the windows
      and killed the grass.
Inside the house is Ruth

      eyes blue as a woman's I saw yesterday in the street
      perhaps this is what reminds me.
Why didn't you call me, says Ruth.

I thought of the divorce,
my mother in the hospital with the faded blue blanket,
      the man who sat in his car
      outside my house in the dusk.
Ruth showed me the yard, filled with weeds and
      dandelions gone to seed

———

soon there will be English peas, runner beans and squash,
baby lettuces edged with Queen Anne's lace.

> Once in a fishing store I looked at a map of Canada
> and saw her town—Thunder Bay—
> I always liked the sound of it.

There's a kind of basil that smells like Meyer lemon—
> last night I used it when I cooked basmati rice.
> The way the lemon's skin feels smooth
> like the skin of a lover,
> scented with something from far away

> lemon that glows like light
> shines through the edges of my fingers
> not memory but a beacon

How we find ourselves, walk down a street in surprise.
Wondering, have we seen this place before?
Sun breaking up morning gloom
smell of good salt—
> I taste it on my skin and later
> on strawberries that come from the garden.
Why didn't you call me, she says, all these years.

Do you hear me?

About Emory

I like to think that Heaven is a lush green place, on
    the other side of a wide blue river.
My old dog runs free in the long grass
    even her muzzle freshly dark;
my mother is there too, hair curly and clean
    like the color of sun when I was a child.
    She wears a dress I remember: dropped waist with
    narrow bands of blue.
I see my friend Emory who died just three days ago as well,
    he picnics with a group of Belgian scholars
    on a white lace cloth,
    they eat sandwiches and chicken breast
    with basil and cherry.

Everyone. My husband's grandmother and
    my father. Later he walks over,
    wears the same grey slippers,
    carries a pitcher of perfect martinis,
    raises one to his lips.
Light fractures in the blue glass.

But it gets complicated.
    The ex-boyfriend my mother never could stand
    will be there too,
    and my former sister-in-law—the one who left
    with the garage mechanic;
    all locked together in perpetual paradise.
    Frankly, it's hard to imagine.

    Still I dance across a field of lost socks,
    a single jacket left once, draped over a chair
    and mourned,

the aquamarine ring my grandfather gave me—
I lost it when I was four,
the boy I knew when I was twenty
who wore only white,
even my father's old
Rambler American station wagon
the only new car he ever bought,
he uses it now to trundle roses
and rare gin in paradise.

Are such things still possible? My mother teaches
samba steps to a thin-boned old lady, and
gold and white Queen Anne's lace
blooms freely by the water.

I'd like to think so.
Loss has its own insistence. The heaviness of wood,
the way the body
becomes only spent fabric.
Uncertainty leaves an acrid taste in the mouth.

I am left only with words from the last time I met you,
coffee at the end of lunch,
beneath a white tree dripping blossom
on a pale afternoon in early spring.

Andrea's Wedding (Thinking about La Rubia)

Outside Madrid, a girl with stick-thin legs, tow-headed,
        plays in the pasture. She wants to fight the bulls.

        This is not allowed.
        She practices the postures, moves her feet delicately
        in the dust. She doesn't know it yet but
        she will be famous,
        later, after the dictator dies.
People will call her the blonde goddess,
        collect the handkerchiefs she has touched, sell
        laces and sweet cookies named after her.

It is strange how our own destinies remain obscure to us.
        And strange too that I think this tonight
        dancing in the blue lights of a garden
        as lost bits of fog waft around us. After the toasts
        and the champagne,
        wanting only for the band to continue
        to play one more song.

        When I was fifteen I drew dark lines around my eyes
        and watched my parents' friends
        do what they called dancing.
        I vowed to skip it in adulthood.

At Andrea's wedding though even the rabbi dances,
        her mother and aunts and
        the brother she hasn't seen for years.
        Someone else announces cake, but we keep moving.
Who knows when we will feel this way again?

In Madrid even the bullfighters dance.
And further away, by the shore,

where fishermen pull up
sweet scallops and briny shrimp
and thin tourists sip vermouth
and make their own choreography.

My friend Andrea wears white lace,
her hair curls like a gypsy's.
Once she wanted to die over a man and now,
look at her. Dancing and in love.
All the things we fear—
The blond goddess told no one but
she was secretly afraid of dogs,
and even domestic farm animals.
The cattle with their broad sides and hoofs.

She wanted only to wear a silk jacket
with embroidered sleeves.
A cape seemed like a fine thing.
Her mother had dressed her small brother in silks
when he was far too young.
Something about it irked the girl.

I myself wore a flounced dress,
all red shades and magenta to Andrea's wedding.
The garden was hung with nasturtium and lily.
And later, after the salmon and wine,
my feet moved on the parquet dance floor
not stopping even for the dissolving moon.

One by one the lights were extinguished and finally
only a small trail of blue could be seen
edging the sea.

Just This

This is all I ever wanted
I thought today as I walked in the white light,
strange for February.
I see another woman
 climb over the sharp breakwater to collect
purple anemone in a small metal pail.

The way the tide goes out, leaving hard ridges on the gray
sand--

I remember so clearly being nineteen, thinking
I will get a job selling flowers,
three or four hours a day maybe, the rest of the time
just sit on the beach,
trailing ranunculus and lilies.
I wanted this light,
I wanted it spilling like honey on a clean wood floor,
and music, maybe Joni Mitchell or jazz,
good coffee with cream or maybe later a glass of
some local wine.

A boy rides by on his skateboard,
a woman holds new strawberries
they sit in a pale butter-colored bowl.

Wind chimes sound like the sun on a fine day.

Just this.

The Astronaut

She was always a good girl,
the first with her hand in the air,
in math she covered the answers with her palm,
        so the other kids couldn't cheat.

Some girls spent prom night in the local Ramada Inn,
pouring vodka and red-shaded energy drinks over ice,
colors dancing in the frayed lamp beams like fresh galaxies,
the new gossamer dresses mere cloud on a convenient chair.

But the astronaut girl came home early,
she had an important test.
        The next morning, in her spare moments she
        memorized the table of elements, planned a new way
        to arrange the data.
An earnest valedictorian, her hair
        didn't come out right that day, too short, too curly.
        She tried not to mind,
        exhorted her classmates to
        reach anyway for the stars.
        I knew this girl, once

The astronaut girl flew in the navy vault of sky,
        watched the way light fell,
        the way earth days passed in real hours.
        She also watched the large hands of the pilot.
        People said he had a way with women.
        She wondered what this meant as
        she operated the robotic arm of the ship,
        pulsing outward into that black yaw of space.

And in four months she knew he didn't really love her.
It's just one of those things, the pilot said.
        What could you expect,

———

flying past the moon and all.
She left her three children, her white mini van,
her big brick house
in the best part of the suburbs,

drove all night, nine hundred miles,
not even stopping to use the facilities,
to squirt a thin spray of pepper juice in the eyes of her rival.
It was her own eyes she wanted to close.

She believed everything they told her. That
a man's reach must exceed his grasp,
that the sky was a plum-sheeted slice of paper,
that night would explode outside the window of the
cosmos in never to be repeated patterns of
undisclosed light.
That love would come like that too.

She was the smartest girl in the school;
she would soar like a rocket,
over all the white houses and cookie sales
sky shifting from sable to pale lines of ash,
she would fly over everything

exempt always from gravity.

*Note: In 2007 NASA astronaut Lisa Nowak was arrested,
reportedly in a wig and diapers after driving over 900
miles in her mini-van to attack her rival in a love triangle.
Newspapers asserted that she was involved in a
clandestine relationship with her pilot, and he did, in fact,
later, marry Nowak's rival. Her career was terminated by
NASA and her own husband left her.*

Tonight I Read Old Kerouac

after

tonight I read old Kerouac again
        —stumbling tumbling always against that line—
        accept loss forever
I mean, I know, it's just Jack doing that Buddhist thing
        saying accept it, deal with it,
        get over it,
        it's all gone
        or going
        disengage—detach
        it all goes—we are as grass under our feet

only I don't believe he got over it,
        ever let go
        let loss play over him like a freak silver storm
        like a lover tracing the slim shape of a rib
        then gone
in the end Jack with his liquor and bennies
        living with his mother in Florida
        couldn't do it either.

Add up the total—the umber of my father's voice
        the too soft white face of my dog,
        the way she'd lean into my knees
        just when we think we've learned detachment
        the word falls into silence

        I recall the color of sky in 1988
        in Los Angeles,
                the fall smelled of sunlight and carob

I see instead my dog running with
three coyotes up the bank near the old lake
come home to herself

the way birds at the top of a tree flutter at once
making the whole world sound wind and air
the way thin light falls in late October
breaking into braille across our hands,

saying always, hold this.

After a Bicycle Theft

My brother's wife is leaving—
      packing her grandmother's French luggage,
      taking the silver and
      giving serious consideration
      to the waxed blond wood dining table.
I saw her last in July,
      she wore a white jogging jacket,
      we'd just eaten breakfast—
      whole-wheat toast with honey, good coffee,
      read the paper,
      she went out for a run.
      It seems she was already gone

In November the light thins,
earth turns away on its axis,

my Buddhist friends tell me:
      things change.

But I'm sick of change,
of things breaking,
      the cabinet that now needs repair,
      the frail trunk of a young peach tree
      snapped like a white neck
by the persistent santa ana wind,
      whipping even the thorny blossoms of bougainvillea.

Sitting in comfortable leather chairs, smooth as butter, or
      in line at the supermarket counting change,
      holding fat brown pears in our hands,

      we sit in the foreshortened days
      waiting for loss.

———

Again.

Or watching a faded L.A. skyline
through windows,
remark on the clean parquet of the floor,
pure polished oak
against the clean glass.
We think about the color white,
        tell one another
        we are safe.

Collection

My brother's first wife smoked incessantly,
  her red lipstick marked gray-blue stubs and
once she blew smoke, purposely, into my mother's face.
We had all traveled somewhere up the coast,
  stood together on a sloped wooden balcony.

She was very thin, that woman.
Three days past Christmas
  she left a scarf at my house,
  I never saw her again and
  I kept it.
  Fake leopard silken and long,
  kept it not for any sentimental reason,
  just something.

Much later my brother married again,
strawberry blond hair, she stood taller than any of us,
I liked to look at her hands—smooth like a child's.

She fixed us toast and strong coffee,

in the valley out behind the house
  light mixed with fog
  everything was gray.

Now she's gone too.
  I didn't have a chance to take anything of hers,
  but I would have,
  maybe a small string of agate beads
  brought from Brazil,
  a ring, or even
  one of the lace doilies she brought back from France.

We meet people and think there's some connection,
        the way our hands touch, that things last,
        that we will all know each other when we're old.
        The last night of high school three of us promised to
        meet in twenty-five years.

I forget where.
We think we will keep something
        and perhaps we are right.

Tonight at my brother's birthday party,
as the white smoke of candles
        reaches in gray arabesques toward sky,
        I place a small spoon in my pocket.

Wind Flapping Like Broken Wings

Warm winds roll through the canyon today
brown leaves, the broken limbs of trees and dust,
spilled bougainvillea,
     a lost trashcan in my backyard.
I think of my father.

The year I was five he made me a butterfly costume
read at some length from the Encyclopedia Britannica
about the habits of the monarch—
how it waited on a slim wire of branch, paused and
pulsed its wings slowly.
He heated thin strips of bamboo cut from a hedge in the yard.
   All dichondra
 and rainbird sprinklers
he liked to sit out in the hot fall nights
in the rhythmic sound of water
a glass of bourbon and ice in his hand.
And later he painted the gauze wings, replicated patter
told me to stand still in front of each spectator and flutter,
each wing taller and more substantial than I.

There are other stories
   about my father and bourbon
   less happy stories that
   I stand in the hot wind and disregard.

In the riverbed beneath my house
   coyotes lap at the trickle of green water
   a man plays a trumpet far away behind the trees
   first scales, then a song
   sound rich and full
   like a lost voice in a dream that is finally telling a truth

today in the brown fall.
I make list
use a rough brush to clean cobwebs
make plans: a holiday, a party I must give for my daughter
the lean line of a man's torso

when the wind stops with what are we left?

The spill of petals across grass
and the small hum of insects
flickering through green vine.

Watching Films in the Nursing Home

My mother-in-law places a six of spades
      on a red five of hearts
      fingers splayed, big table covered with magazines,
      Kleenex,
      an empty ice cream dish.
Les, her new friend, hints at good card plays
 Tom, neck in a brace,
      just nods from too many pain killers while
      his wife reads aloud from a travel magazine.
      I like to be home before dark, she tells me

      before she leaves, bending down, whispering
      next summer they'll be in Tucson
      some place where it stays light late.

But it's evening now, dusk flickers at the windows,
two women on the flowered upholstered couch, uneasy.

They know about night, but say little
      Instead they nibble on popcorn,
      moving the exploded kernels
      with unsteady hands.

We want to leave.

But then, everyone wants to go.

My husband finds a television hidden inside an armoire
      like in some fancy motel
      we all watch a movie
      about a king who could not speak

we cannot understand the others characters,
faces and voices blurred
Tom reads the captions
while we sit with our snacks,

all of us watching the dark grey sky peering
through the spaces between drapes and glass.

Remembering

and mute.

III   Four Oaks at the End of the Mind

The Four Oaks at the End of the Mind

I used to sit beneath a gaudy umbrella
at the Four Oaks Café, on the outskirts of Los Angeles
      glass full of champagne, nineteen,
      eating eggs Florentine,
chunks of wheat toast spread with orange marmalade.
The couples on the shaded balcony above the street
remind me.

One of my friends wants us all to buy the café.
We'd serve Marseilles-style bouillabaisse,
      beef and mushroom stew,
      apple tartin;
      all the nearly famous hipsters would arrive,
      as well as a woman in white who'd play the harp.

Today on these yellowed coastal hills oaks grow thick.
Sumac and pale grass spread under foot,
mix with faded nasturtium.
Limbs and leaves make a canopy.
There's a man and a woman I've seen, often, walking
upward
to hide under the black silhouette of tree.

My friend married his second wife
      in an isle of cypress and old wood.
A tall and supple red-head, she left,
      a trail of alcohol fumes and smashed glass.
      Be careful, I say to him now. But he ignores me
      making leg of lamb with saffron and crab salad
for a line of thin, well turned out women.

———

Here also, so many places named in the same way:
    Oak Grove, Paso Robles,
    Arroyo Robles, Avenue de los Robles.

My husband and I have lunch in a glen
a ruined trunk stands in the field
our palms touch beneath the table.

Let's leave all this, my husband says,
    sail fast in a clean white boat
    away from these complications and
    the incessant rumble of trees

    let us begin again.

Yet under the bright awnings a man serves
deep dishes filled with fresh pasta and truffle jam.
We are ringed by stands of grim oak.
Abruptly a woman drops her glass to the ground,

    and ruined light sputters into the last final
filaments of fall.

Arborist

Ten years ago a young man decided to climb
the world's highest redwood, decided to climb without ropes,
  swinging free from trunk to limb,
  body swaying like cloth or frail cloud.
His girlfriend said he was in love with trees,
  more than with her, really.
He sat some days just staring up,
  watching the thick crown of branches form a shadow,
  watching the sky move, turn different shades,
  become finally black.
At home the girl fixed dinner,
opened a bottle of cheap wine, waited,
wondered if this was how it would always be.

My father wanted to spend summers
  staring at those trees too.
Although it wasn't summer really,
just the two weeks he had off.
We'd look at the same trees,
  sometimes he'd try to draw them.
  The thickness of trunk,
  the way they'd move up into space,
  scraping the sky with soft bark,
  as if there was some new way to be in the world.

My mother grew bored by the trees,
the spongy dirt piled beneath them.
  I went alone with my father.
  I remember the smell still,
  like salt and sawdust shot through with rot,
  the way the ground was warm.
  Later he'd drink bourbon,
  lie down in the tent and sleep,

dreaming I think of trees.

When the man trims the trees along the street today,
        I remember that smell.
        My father was from the Midwest,
        those trees were different;
        and my mother from Brazil—
        the trees there had immense flat leaves,
        wet and very green
        like the wings of parrots in a hot rain,

not like these trees.

The young man climbing wants to believe in something,
        wants to know why
        the sky becomes shaped like an ellipsis,
        to understand that particular dark color of green, and
        how the thick barrel-shaped limbs
        resemble the body of his father.

He stays in the trees for a long time
        even after his arms tire and
        the light fades.

In the Valley of the Amazon

In the cheese and wine shop
the man behind the counter
listens to Bruce Springsteen,
  and wraps the pale sheep's milk cheese in blue paper.
In another corner of the store a man
wears a faded baseball cap and drinks wine.
He talks with the faded brunette who works the bar—
  tells her how it feels, now, after his wife left.
  She took his daughter
  and all the kitchen appliances and
  the dust accumulates on the coffee table
  and on the stand next to his bed.
He says he's just tasting but
his third glass of wine stands empty.

Far away in the jungle of northern Brazil a small band
  Of natives shoot arrows at planes that fly over,
  hide beneath leaves that are
  green and broad as parrots.
  They've never seen roads or movies, or even
  the place where their wide river meets the sea,
  and dark fingers of mud move
  for miles into the salt water.

They don't want to see these things either, or
  at least, that's what the paper says, and
  I can't help but think they're probably right.
The cheese man turns up the volume and asks
  if I want to buy that New York Times.

I've been the girl in that song.
  shot my own arrows upward toward the arched sky
  hoping to prevent what I can't even name

----

the same words the man with the baseball cap
writes at home in the dust on the table.
He whispers it now to the tired brunette.
She's shot her own quiver of arrows by now,
    —her first husband, she runs into him still, and the
    boyfriend who used her credit card
    (he claimed it was an accident) and
    even the cheese man
    (with whom she's had a few rounds)

slowly she nods her head, pours another glass
    plum colored and full to the brim.

Remembering Sean

I think it was the way the bones of his face were carved
    almost exposed, almost painful.
In fact it must have hurt—the way his face was shadowed,
    never smiled, eyes smudged.
I wouldn't mention him today except for a boy I saw,
          a man really.
          He and his wife were fixing up a scuttled boat
          and you could tell money was a problem.
          They met in high school, the man said.
          In Santa Maria.
          She'd married someone else and
          it all went bad pretty fast.
The girl was dark, a little plump.
          Her ex-husband had taken the kids.
          I waved at the two of them as
          they motored away in a dented dinghy
          in a cloud of engine exhaust.

Anyway, it was his face that reminded me.

And once at the market
          the guy bagging my groceries.
          The same look, freckles, lost, a little bewildered.
          Sun-streaked hair.

  You can tell they all surf, these boys
          looking to the ocean
          to give back something they once lost.

I want to tell them the sea never returns anything.

The boy I knew told me about a girl,
          how he'd crashed a car at work,

---

never finished anything.
Hapless.

I wouldn't remember now
     except for the dream where
     we meet of course on the beach.
There's a shock too in seeing his face on someone else.

Those sad boys, all fluid movement
     they haven't learned yet how to be tough,
     to realize the grace of riding a wave
     will find but slim remuneration.

Still they persist.

Even today, the fog thick and heavy, nearly August
     the beach cheerless
     sand like a fine white powder
     I trace all the names I can't remember

watch a thin boy in a wetsuit, deep eye sockets and stern

he rides the last waves in an empty world.

Listening to Coltrane

That Friday night, after steaks and
    a grilled white fish translucent as pearl,
    the dry French cheese made from sheep's milk,
    green beans and
    dates the shade of mahogany,
after all that we sat by the fire and listened to Coltrane.

It was late then and we were quiet,
my husband smoked a good cigar and
my brother closed his eyes and looked toward the ceiling.
    His wife had been gone then for seven weeks,
    the sound came through the big clean room like
    Coltrane himself was there, hitting the notes,
    Saying this is all there is. It's all loss and
    the wonder of thick stars in a cold sky.
Sluice it with Scotch or anything else, just hear that sound,
    all saxophone and mahogany.

We knew too that later, on other nights,
    there'd be parties, even dancing.
    Women's stiletto heels here on the thin parquet,
    a woman with black hair and a green jacket,
    that we'd sat together on
    a thousand evenings like this.
    Once off the old canals in Venice,
    we'd barbequed among
    the stray cats and the yellow grass and
    the scent of sea.

That night as we listened to the music
we knew we'd passed into some new place,
we were no longer children.
We examined the redwood and

---

steel girders of the rebuilt deck,
the way sound passed through the body, how it came
through the hardwood floor
and into the soles of the feet, the palms of the hands,
caught at the throat and then twisted off into the smoky haze
of night.

The house felt empty, the cat and
the silver and the bright coverlet
that once covered the bed in the guest room,
all gone.

Maybe I should wash the dishes, I thought, and then
I turned to talk about politics, perhaps, or art, or the late
hour,
		to ask some question possibly even about love.

But it didn't matter.
The room was filled with sound,
a balloon of amber colored light rising steadily,
and we held our fingers upward to the fire so the light shone
through them
and we listened.

IV My Mother's Parrot

My Mother's Parrot

The thing is, I'll never know the parrot's name.
How he called to my mother—
Maria Thereza, café, obrigada—
(yes, he drank coffee, swore in Portuguese and in Dutch),
spread his chartreuse wings
like some thin imported silk,
in my grandfather's kitchen in Santos,
where women in white
threw flowers on New Year's into the sea.

The parrot's name will be like the samba,
something I never learned.
There's no translation possible,
lost now on the wrong side of the equator.
When my father mixed gin and vermouth, bellicose voiced,
my mother closed the windows, stopped
speaking English,
watched telenovelas without sound and then
Bruin basketball.
At lunch I tell my friend we all speak an indecipherable code,
we know nothing of one another. Drink your wine, she says.
And I do.
Outside a big-winged bird dips from the sky, parrot green.

The Beginning

On that day when he rode inland from the port of Santos,
(later they would plant sugar cane, later he would think
differently)
the pampas grass reached as high as the chest of a man
          on horseback.
Later people would speak of other things,

but that day he thought only of a certain shade of green.
Green like the low blades of grass, close to the root,
like the vast wings of birds taking flight together
so the sky became a map of cerulean,
he would remember that.

Because later things would change,
as things do.

But that day he took off his helmet,
          let his hands hang and his horse stop walking.
Green, he thought, like water welling up from the trough of
river,
          green as emerald, green as hope
          when you are too young to know,
green as light.

The green you've known too,
          even now,
          though much has happened.
That you sang to me, seated on a bench in a bar,
that was green too.

And when he sat on his horse, let his hands fall until

they were hidden in grass,
when all the words he knew
were words for green,
like the sounds of small insects,
like the broad fronds falling across sky from trees,
all green,
he knew.

What My Mother Learned Later

The two-headed white snake lives under the banana tree,
      lolling beneath broad green leaves, eating sweet fruit.
The woman who came from the north—
      from Bahia—to cook told her this.
She didn't care, she ate bananas too,
      mashed with rice for her dinner,
      and the small apple-tasting ones outside
      in back of the one remaining barn.

Here too she rolled corn silk into cigarette papers,
waited for the end of the world.

In the meantime she learned to embroider—
      tea clothes and napkins.
Later in life, on another continent,
she would examine her stitches,
      shake her head.
In the land of the blind
the one-eyed man is king, she told me.
Here you can't even find good coffee.

The two-headed snake ate bananas and told her fortune,
      counseled patience,
      told her to learn to play the guitar—
      samba or fado, to play alone.
      But she had long thin feet,
      wanted to dance and would not listen.

We all receive warnings: don't marry that man—he drinks
      and he's an angry drunk.
Go south or east
      or any other direction that will take you away.
Leave now.

———

She fed the snake an apple scented with smoke, and
        told him not to worry.

Her eyes were very blue.

She would eat liquor-flavored candies and
tell the nuns at the Catholic school
        she never smoked.
She copied her friend's homework and
learned American dance steps.

Be careful under fruit trees, she would say, years later.
No one ever listens.

Take Me to Hollywood

In 1943 Clark Gable landed on the docks of Santos, Brazil
—something to do with entertaining the troops
(he thought too of shooting a scene later on in Rio,
pictured himself in white strolling
      along the fine sand of Copacabana).

Schoolgirls in uniforms, all prim pleated skirts,
      dodged the nuns
      and made for the waterfront.
They were used to the ships that floated far away in the bay
      like vast lost birds, or angels,
      because even though Santos was balmy enough still
      they longed for Paris, Manhattan and
      the big lawns in Beverly Hills.

In history class they learned about Crazy Maria,
      the phony queen.
      Deposed after Napoleon she sailed away
      back to the continent,
      threw all her slippers—
      even the red velvet ones with three inch heels,
      even the jewel-encrusted dance shoes
      made by an artisan in Italy—
threw them all in the water behind her.
She would not carry the dust of the colonies home, she said.
The girls laughed but secretly wanted those shoes and
      to dance bare foot over the water like Crazy Maria.

On the way to the docks they practiced singing:

      Clark Gable, Clark Gable; take me to Hollywood.
      They believed in jacaranda and a new kind of light.

———

Clark Gable saw them, thin-armed girls dancing
against the blue Brazilian sea,
girls who drank dark cafezinhos and
threw flowers along the shore.

My mother told me this story.

Her friends said she looked like Rita Hayward.
        She wanted to play the guitar and sing fados
        but her father wouldn't let her.
All dead now—Clark Gable, my mother,
        her best friend Letticia.

So much of our lives we see things one way
        until some sudden reversal.

Yet we continue to think of the sea
—of a certain shade of white sand and
some polished stone on a particular stretch of beach.

Looking always to find some representation of light
recalled only slightly or perhaps merely dreamed.

Cologne

The last time I saw my mother's house,
      the day the sale was final,
I stood in the thick green of the shiny leaved orange tree
      let twigs scratch my arms while I
      picked every single piece.
      They were Spanish, blood oranges,
      fragrant still of some other place
      —almost any place might be better—
I moved two cinderblocks, climbed high,
      made certain I found each fruit,
      filled three boxes.

Everyday I peel a few,
know when they're gone, it's final.

Inside, empty, the house seemed smaller.
I always thought bare buildings would be bigger,
wash of green curtains over bleached oak,
      the five sets of china,
      the wind chimes.
Dinner on Sunday, two kinds of meat and fruit salad,
thin smoke from my mother's ashtray
rising blue-tinged and acrid,
made the house bigger.
Now empty,

just the light falls, like an empty sleeve,
like my mother's thin body seemed bigger.
And then, after they took off the mask,
there was nothing left, only flesh without breath.

Late at night I pull out the red plaid shirt she wore.
I saved it, still freshly pressed,
bury my face in the darkness.

 Tonight I shopped for perfume.
Pale pink, the bottle carved glass and squat,
all rose oil and organdy, clean grass
way too much money. I hid the receipt.
My skin smells
like my mother,
the summer I turned sixteen.

I did it my way

I saw today that Al Viola died—
        not that I knew who he was until I read the caption.
        He used to play guitar with Frank Sinatra.
        I did it my way was our song, he said,
        and for twenty-five years he'd played
        along with Frank.

It's about Heaven that I wonder.
Picture that scene: Frank standing at a craps table—
        in Heaven your number always comes up—
        drumming his fingers, cigarette smoke wafting,
        eyes bluer than ever.
He shakes his head, mumbles that after all,
        the guy just played back up, and here he is,
        late again.
        We thought you'd never get here, Frank tells Al
        and sets him up with the Rat Packers
        at some celestial table,
still telling bad jokes, still
clicking ice cubes in glasses of single malt Scotch.

The last time Frank played Vegas I regret
I didn't pack up my mother,
take all her heart medications and just drive.
Afterwards we could have played a few slots,
maybe had lunch at Caesar's
        or even the Hacienda.

I wonder if those old headliners still open in the hereafter.
        If they do, my mother's there for sure.
There's so much about death I don't understand:
        How is it Heaven if we're stuck with our same selves?
        And if we're not there at all, what does it matter?

———

The article said Al's survived by children and grandchildren.
Did they take him out into the Valley for brunch?
        Like all old people he'd have to be careful
        with salt and sugar and potassium.
        I used to steal blueberry muffins
        and olives from the buffet for my mother.
She wasn't supposed to have them but one day you figure,
what's the point.
She'd tilt her head and listen to the music
coming from the speaker in the corner
and sing along.
Mother, I'd say, we're in a restaurant.
That's Frankie, she said.

There's so much we think we know but really
there's just the music and the restaurant and
the light leaking in around the heavy drapes,
falling in patterns on the veneered table,
the sound of silver hitting glassware,
light falling all around us and somewhere, on a Sunday,
someone keeps time with a spoon
to a song most of us can't even hear.

Little Church

They called it making the little church—
when the priest would take a bottle or two of good wine,
      a few cruzeiros from the collection plate and
      secret them away.
      Within the chapel maybe, but more likely
      in the small, shabby house,
      just next to the parish office.
Each week he'd add to his hoard, sometimes at night
counting the coins, looking at the dates on the bottles,
      thinking how the islands off the coast of Portugal
      must have looked that season.
      Thinking about what he'd lost,
      swirling the red wine, saying this is my blood.

My mother taught me this.
A kind of cookie hidden in a tin,
      tissue-thin nightgowns, tags still attached--
      a box of antique silver spoons,
      a wooden case filled with guavas.
It's something you keep just for yourself, she said,
      something too rare and fine.
We gave away all her clothes, somewhere
      someone finds a stash of hand-embroidery and bills.
I have my own cache now—lace lingerie stacked,
      a certain secret account,
      a shoebox and a small sequined bag
      filled with spare change—

not for any real purpose, only against the dark, against the
      always possible and the ceaselessness of desire.

All the nights the priest sat alone, his skin hot and untouched,
when the cheap leather of his shoes hurt his feet and

> the air in the church was thick and fetid.
> He'd touch the cool glass of the bottles, know
> he still had something,
> could claim some special place,
> touching the tips of his fingers together,
> making the little church.

A Genealogy

It may be that you are like that first man
      who rode on a fat pony across the pampas grass.
Today you watch the skyline of city grow jagged black
against morning,
the small sounds of your car—it is blue and fast—
      make you nervous but still, you go on.
Because like that man you feel hope,
      and in its absence even obligation.

In your house which is nearly all glass you pour a drink,
      hear the sound of ice cubes,
      the blue of your pool is the same blue of paper
      that children receive to wrap gifts.

Our mother told us about that man on horseback,
      that we are like him.

Of course there are stories: that the man was seduced
      away from the earth by emeralds.
      In the end, he kept them in a bag by his head
      while he slept.
      I do not know if this is true.
      They say he killed his own son,
      something about the hands of the boy's mistress.
      They were so fine.
      She was a native,
      her breasts bare and small like the fruit
      that grows now behind the house of our cousin.

I don't think these stories matter.

The ground felt new to that man—soft, grassy
and the air marked with some original light.

This is why all of us in our family collect birds
        or at least slim prisms of glass.

It may be that you are like him,
        as you sit in a club along Hollywood Boulevard,
        visit a wine merchant, or
        shop for a suit from an English tailor.
Not because of these things.

But because it is about light and the little sounds of morning.
Because you still believe
that something can be found and made new.

Acknowledgements:

I need to offer a profound thank you to: Mark Smith for envisioning this project and then making certain that the vision actually found expression, to Trish and Rick Cornez for years of support and for Trish's detailed art and web work, to Benjamin Hatheway for his creative web, cover, manuscript and design work and for dealing with the many vast mysteries of computer technology, to Samantha Smith for reminding me why we do this, to Paul Rohrer who figures in many of the poems, to Steven McDonald—colleague, dean and friend—who kept bringing me back to poetry, to Kevin Williams who really does sail Kevin's boat, to all the people who sail on that boat, and, of course, always, to Carlton Smith for reading, editing, discussing and believing.

Deborah Paes de Barros grew up in Southern California, haunted by the sounds of swamp coolers and the frequent Santa Ana winds. She is Professor of English and an occasional and rather nervous sailor. Her work has appeared in a number of poetry and literary journals and she is also the author of *Fast Cars and Bad Girls.*